Italian Futurism

The First Modern Avant-Garde Movement

Rosemary K. West

Italian Futurism: The First Modern Avant-Garde Movement
Dark Cat Books, Los Angeles

Copyright © 2015, Rosemary K. West

ISBN-13: 978-1517037796
ISBN-10: 1517037794

Contents

Introduction

The early 20th century is often referred to as an age of isms. There was a great proliferation of political, literary and artistic movements throughout Europe, all aimed at changing some aspect of society. There were so many of these ideas all emerging and developing in such a short period, that today we often just lump them together under the heading of modernism.

But for some people, modernization just wasn't happening fast enough. A group of Italian writers and artists who called themselves Futurists were frustrated by the sense that Italy was stuck in the past. They felt that Italian culture was stagnating, still resting on accomplishments that dated back to the Renaissance.

So they decided to shake things up. In 1909 they published the first Futurist manifesto, announcing a movement that would emphasize speed, technology, youth, defiance and violence.

Equating museums and libraries with cemeteries, calling for the destruction and rebuilding of cities, and demanding the removal of pasta from the Italian cuisine, Futurism was positioned as a total rejection of the past with the goal of replacing nearly all of contemporary culture with a completely original design for the future.

Who Were the Futurists?

There were many writers, artists and others who were actively involved in the Futurist movement. Here are some who were among the most prominent during the early years.

F.T. (Filippo Tommaso) Marinetti was born in 1876 in Alexandria, Egypt to Italian parents. Receiving his early education at a school run by French Jesuits, he began writing poetry in French and founded a literary magazine in order to publish his work [1]. He received his baccalaureate degree at the Sorbonne and then went to Italy to study law. He received his doctorate in 1899, but never practiced law. Upon his father's death in 1907, he inherited a large family fortune. In 1923 he married the artist Benedetta Cappa (1897-1977). They had three daughters.

As a student, Marinetti collaborated on various literary journals, wrote critical essays and articles, and saw some of his poetry published in reputable literary magazines. His first major published poem was "Conquest of the Stars," which was recited by actress Sarah Bernhardt in her Paris salon [2]. After graduating, he continued his literary career as a playwright, poet and critic, and became part of a group of like-minded writers and artists in Milan who were developing a new artistic philosophy. As described by Günther Berghaus:

> They proclaimed the cultural bankruptcy of a nation that clung to the past and ignored the great advances of the modern world. They ridiculed the ossified cultural and political institutions, the servile respect paid to an intellectual and artistic cult of the glorious Italian past. Instead, they sought nothing less than to revolutionize life and society in all their diverse aspects: moral, artistic, cultural, social, economic, and political[3].

Marinetti's initial Futurist manifesto was published in the Parisian newspaper *Le Figaro* in February 1909. During the next three years, Marinetti and his colleagues would publish at least thirty more manifestos along with many letters, articles, broadsheets and pamphlets, detailing their theories and ideas.

In keeping with Futurism's glorification of war, Marinetti joined demonstrations encouraging Italy to enter the first World War. He developed a friendship with Benito Mussolini, apparently after the two were arrested together at a pro-war demonstration[4]. When Italy entered the war, Marinetti and many other Futurists enlisted. Although Marinetti served in combat, he was permitted, unlike a typical soldier, to come and go from the war zone, and he traveled throughout Italy giving lectures and performing in Futurist theater productions[5].

After the war, Marinetti became more deeply involved with politics. The Futurist Party entered into a coalition with the newly-formed Fascist Party. But at the same time many Futurist Party members were also socialists or sympathetic toward socialist and communist groups; the party relied on support from the working class and leftist factions. Marinetti was elected to the central committee of the Fascist Party in 1919, but was unsuccessful as a parliamentary candidate[6]. Around this time he described Mussolini as a "megalomaniac who will little by little become a reactionary"[7]. Mussolini began distancing himself from left-wing groups, and the Futurist Party began to dissolve as its members either joined other parties or moved away from politics. Marinetti resigned from the Fascist central committee in 1920 and returned to promoting Futurism as a cultural and social movement, although he never lost his interest in politics.

The cultural activities of the Futurists had languished during the war. Marinetti sought to revitalize the movement, starting with a conversion of the Futurist Party's newspaper from a political to an artistic journal. Between 1920 and 1924, a series

4

of publications, performances and exhibitions helped attract many new artists to a "second wave" of Futurism[8].

At the same time, Mussolini was in the process of silencing and eliminating the left-wing and anti-Fascist groups in Italy. Survival required compromise. In 1923, Marinetti published *Manifesto to the Fascist Government*, in which he emphasized that Mussolini alone would run the political operations of Italy, while Futurism would remain autonomous in the field of art[9]. But his independence was really an illusion. In 1929 he became a member of the new Italian Academy[10], the very kind of institution he had spent so much of his career condemning. Although not much was left of the Futurist movement, it was for many years one of the very few forums in which the creative community still had some opportunities for innovation and expression. But it was increasingly under attack, and in 1939 its newspaper was shut down, to be replaced by a government-controlled publication[11]. This effectively ended what little was left of Futurism as a creative movement.

Despite his personal misgivings about Mussolini, despite his problems with government censorship, and despite the end of the artistic vision to which he had devoted himself for so long, Marinetti remained loyal to the Fascist government. He had seen first-hand the horrors of the first World War and its devastating aftereffects in Europe, yet he never lost his enthusiasm for war and the Italian military. At age 60 he served as an officer in the Ethiopian campaign (1935-36), and during World War II, in his late sixties, he volunteered for the Russian front. He continued to produce writings which were by now almost entirely government propaganda, such as the poem "I Sing the Heroes and Machines of Mussolini's War," espousing heroic patriotism and modern warfare[12]. He died of a heart attack in Bellagio, Italy, in December 1944.

Umberto Boccioni was born in Italy in 1882. Along with Gino Severini, he studied for a time with Giacomo Balla, then a proponent of Divisionism, an Italian variation of neo-Impressionism[13]. All three men would eventually become part of the Futurist movement.

In 1907 Boccioni moved to Milan, where he continued to experiment with different painting techniques. There he became acquainted with Marinetti and joined the Futurists. His large painting, *The City Rises*, was created in 1910.

Boccioni was one of the signers of the 1910 "Futurist Painting: Technical Manifesto" which declared that "universal dynamism must be rendered in painting as a dynamic sensation"[14]. Several of the paintings he created during the next few years emphasized this idea by including the word "Dynamism" in the titles. He used vibrant colors, intersecting planes and a sometimes three-dimensional appearance to create a sense of movement.

In 1912 he published the "Technical Manifesto of Futurist Sculpture" and in 1913 "The Plastic Foundations of Futurist Sculpture and Painting." His 1913 sculpture, *Unique Forms of Continuity in Space*, is now acknowledged as a masterpiece and is represented on an Italian coin. It was created in plaster, but two bronze casts were made later. His other plaster sculptures have not survived, but are known from photographs. Some additional bronzes and multimedia sculptures have survived and are in museum collections, as are many of his paintings.

In 1915, after Italy had declared war on Austria and Germany, Boccioni was among several leading Futurists who volunteered for military service. He died after falling from his horse during a training exercise in August 1916.

Giacomo Balla was born in Turin, Italy, in 1871. He studied art at several academies and at the University of Turin. By the time he met Boccioni and Severini, he was well-established as a successful artist whose work had been shown at several important exhibits in Europe. He signed the "Manifesto of Futurist Painters" in 1910, and was very active in the movement for several years, creating one of its most recognizable and popular paintings, *Dynamism of a Dog on a Leash*, in 1912. Balla left the Futurist movement during the 1930s and continued painting. He died in Rome in 1958.

Fortunato Depero was born in 1892. He grew up in Rovento, where he attended a technical school. While apprenticed to a marble worker, he began exhibiting his drawings and paintings. After a 1913 trip to Florence, where he discovered writings by the Futurists published in the newspaper *Lacerba*, he allied himself with the movement and moved to Rome. Depero was considered one of the most prolific and versatile of the Futurists, working in the fine arts, literature, music, stage design and costume, choreography, interior design, and fashion. In addition to participating in performances and exhibiting his work with the Futurists, he had many one-man shows in both Europe and the United States. During the 1920s and 30s he had great success in fashion and advertising, both in Italy and New York, designing artwork and covers for magazines, including *Vanity Fair*, *Vogue*, and *The New Yorker*. His 1932 design for the Campari soda bottle is still in production. He died in Rovento in 1960.

Aldo Palazzeschi (pen name of Aldo Giurlani) was born in Florence in 1885. Initially trained in accounting, he took acting lessons and was, briefly, part of a theatrical troupe. His verse and fiction appeared in various Futurist publications, and he was the author of at least one of the manifestos, "Against Sadness"[15]. During World War I, he was drafted into the Italian army, but never served in combat, apparently because of poor health. He disassociated himself from the Futurist movement around 1914. After the war he devoted himself to writing fiction and memoirs, gradually giving up the fantasy and inventiveness that had characterized his previous work, and became quite successful "perhaps . . . because of this more accessible manner"[16]. He died in 1974.

Luigi Russolo, born in 1885, was a painter who came from a "musical family"[17] and became interested in developing a new approach to music. He wrote "The Art of Noises" in 1913 and, working with painter Ugo Piatti, constructed mechanical sound synthesizers called noise intoners (*intonarumori*). Both Russolo and composer Francesco Ballila Pratella created orchestral scores for the instruments. A series of concerts in London and several Italian cities met with occasional positive responses, but overall Russolo's work was not well received.

Like many other Futurists, Russolo enlisted in the army at the beginning of World War I. He received a serious head wound in 1917. After more than a year of recovery, he moved to Paris where he developed new instruments, and continued writing and performing music. He favorably impressed some composers of the time, including Maurice Ravel and Edgard Varèse[18], but was not able to achieve any financial success. He turned from Futurism to mysticism and published a book, *Beyond the Material World*, in 1938. He died in 1947.

All of Russolo's instruments were destroyed when Paris was bombed during World War II, and very few of his scores have survived, some only as fragments. Yet he is acknowledged as an influence on many experimental composers, such as Igor Stravinsky, Arthur Honegger, and John Cage[19]. The 1980s musical group Art of Noise was named as a tribute to Russolo.

Many other people considered themselves Futurists, some for a just few years, others for decades. According to Willard Bohn, Futurism eventually "attracted hundreds of adherents and spread to nearly every corner of Italy"[20].

Futurism and Art

Today the Futurist movement is best remembered for its influence in the art world, particularly in the area of painting. Yet there is often no clear separation between Futurist works and those that fall into other Modernist categories, particularly Cubism. Their philosophies were different, but the end results were remarkably similar. Many critics and art historians view Cubism and Futurism as closely related, sometimes merging, and the term Cubo-Futurism (or Cubofuturism) is often used, especially when referring to works produced after the first few years of both movements.

As art historian Max Kozloff writes: "To speak of Cubism and Futurism is to speak of the art of young men, close contemporaries in Paris and Milan, whose development was almost simultaneous and certainly complementary"[21]. In this context, the Cubists are Pablo Picasso, Georges Braque, Juan Gris, and many other artists who were considered part of the Cubist school during the early part of the 20th century. The Futurists are Umberto Boccioni, Giacomo Balla, Carlo Carrà, Gino Severini, and the other artists who aligned themselves with Futurism during the same period.

By all accounts the Cubists and the Futurists were variously friends, colleagues and spirited rivals whose competition was often fierce. The Futurist artists are typically portrayed as responding to or being inspired by developments introduced by the Cubists, but also coming up with their own innovations.

Kozloff goes on to say that Cubism, unlike many other Modernist movements, was purely about art and the visual world, without specific political or sociological aims. ". . . the Cubists restricted themselves to aesthetic pursuits and were disinclined to advance theoretical claims for their work . . ."[22].

The Futurists, on the other hand, were constantly advancing theories and claims, which were forcefully expressed through their many manifestos and other publications. From the very beginning, they announced their intention to make a complete break with the artistic past, describing museums as cemeteries and suggesting they should be flushed out and the old canvases allowed to float away[23]. In the 1910 "Manifesto of the Futurist Painters," they condemned classicism, tradition and academics and called for the removal of "all themes and subjects which have been used in the past"[24]. The idea that the past must be completely discarded and forgotten in order to make way for freedom and originality would be a dominant theme in all Futurist manifestos.

Having repeatedly explained what they opposed, the Futurists began, in the 1910 "Futurist Painting: Technical Manifesto," to describe what they wanted to do.

> The gesture which we would reproduce on canvas shall no longer be a fixed moment in universal dynamism. It shall simply be dynamic sensation itself.
>
> Indeed, all things move, all things run, all things are rapidly changing . . . . On account of the persistency of an image upon the retina, moving objects constantly multiply themselves; their form changes like rapid vibrations . . . . Thus a running horse has not four legs, but twenty, and their movements are triangular . . . .
>
> To paint a human figure you must not paint it; you must render the whole of its surrounding atmosphere . . . .
>
> The construction of pictures has hitherto been foolishly traditional. Painters have shown us the objects and the people placed before us. We shall henceforward put the spectator in the centre of the picture[25].

The sense of multiplicity and vibration described is exemplified in Balla's 1912 *Dynamism of a Dog on a Leash*, in which the dog's feet and ears, as well as the leash and the human's feet, can be seen in a blur of motion.

The manifesto's authors went on to discuss theories of color and light and to declare that modern painting could not exist without Divisionism (a painting technique that used small brush strokes to create a radiant effect) [26]. They concluded by demanding, "for ten years, the total suppression of the nude in painting"[27]. This last comment, explained as a response to the tediousness of "artists obsessed with the desire to expose the bodies of their mistresses"[28] is often seen as a jab at Cubism, which had been "genetically linked with the study of the nude"[29].

"Dynamism" and "dynamic sensation" are key terms in the Futurist philosophy. Giovanni Lista explains:

> Boccioni would translate the interdependence of body and space into a symbiotic exchange of energy: The Futurist principle of "copenetration" was based on a dynamic and contrasting integration of the figure and the surrounding environment . . . . Futurists attempted to make as explicit as possible each kinetic movement, not to provide a simple mechanical representation, but to make it emblematic of modern life . . . [30].

"Dynamism," "simultaneity," and "plasticity" are all words frequently used in discussions of both Futurist and Cubist works. When applied to Cubism, these terms generally refer to the concept of showing simultaneous, multiple views of an object or scene, often with the use of intersecting planes or by breaking up the subject and reassembling the parts. The important difference is that in Cubism the focus is on static forms, whereas Futurism concentrates on kinetic states.

However, this does not mean that Cubism ignores movement; simply that it addresses a different sort of movement than Futurism. As Umbro Apollonio explains, "What the Cubists confirmed was rather the motion inherent in the representation of an object even in a stationary position, as a result of the tensions to which it is subjected by the outside forces which crowd around it"[31].

Cubist paintings are frequently described as "analytical" and the early Cubist works often used such muted color palettes that they appear monochromatic. The Futurists, in their pursuit of "dynamism," from the very beginning created dramatic-looking paintings that often employed vibrant colors.

Pablo Picasso's 1912 work, *Still Life with Chair-Caning*, is considered the first "deliberately executed collage"[32]. It combined painting with manufactured materials (rope and printed oilcloth) that were pasted to the canvas. It was not long before other artists were experimenting with combinations of materials such as wallpaper, sand, musical scores, magazine clippings, sequins and fiber.

Later that same year, Boccioni developed a concept of Futurist sculpture that would incorporate a variety of modern materials in place of the traditional marble and bronze. He recommended using "twenty different types of materials"[33] in one work and suggested the use of mechanical devices in order to create actual movement.

With the development of collage art, the line between painting and sculpture was increasingly blurred, and so was the line between the visual arts and literature. Marinetti had invented a poetic form called "parole in libertà" or "words-in-freedom."[34] In his experiments with the visual appearance of a printed poem, the ways in which he laid out the words on the page -- at odd angles, overlapping, in different sizes, etc. -- often resembled collages. At the same time, the makers of collages were in the process of using words as artistic elements.

Futurism and Literature

Futurism was "first conceived as a literary movement"[35]. Marinetti was primarily a writer: poet, playwright, novelist, critic and journalist. Both as a writer and as an editor/publisher of his own and others' work, he was hugely prolific throughout most of his career. It is no surprise that all aspects of the Futurist movement were tirelessly announced, described, promoted and documented in print. No matter what aspect of society and culture was being addressed, be it art, fashion, politics, food, sex or literature, there was always a flurry of manifestos, letters, articles and flyers.

Marinetti had begun publication of the literary magazine *Poesia* in 1905. He published works by many contemporary French poets and internationally recognized writers including Gustave Kahn, Charles Swinburne and William Butler Yeats, along with a large number of young Italian poets who became part of the Futurist movement. Kahn claimed to be the originator of the free verse (*vers libre*) movement[36], which had begun late in the 19th century and was popular with the French Symbolists. The free verse style, which is still a dominant style in poetry today, manipulates the rhythms of natural speech rather than relying on formal meter and rhyme. Marinetti published and wrote free verse, but he would eventually attempt to replace it with his new words-in-freedom approach.

In his 1912 "Technical Manifesto of Futurist Literature"[37], Marinetti called for the banishment of adjectives and adverbs. Verbs would be used only in the infinitive. Nouns would be paired based on perceived associations or analogies. Punctuation would be replaced by mathematical symbols and musical notation. Writers would attempt to express smells, noises and the power of objects. Expectations of rhythm and beauty would be cast aside as

14

poets entered "the boundless domains of free intuition. After Free Verse, here at last we have Words-in-Freedom!"[38].

This manifesto was used as the introduction to the movement's first major poetry collection, *I poeti futurisiti*, even though all the poems in that volume were free verse. According to Zbigniew Folejewski[39], while a few of the poems still included traditional subjects, particularly references to nature, many others focused on some of the modern themes advocated by Marinetti: speed, electricity, space travel and the rejection of tradition. And at least one writer, Aldo Palazzeschi, had started experimenting with the introduction of noise by using onomatopoetic words.

Marinetti expanded on the words-in-freedom concept in his 1913 article, "Destruction of Syntax - Untrammeled Imagination - Words-In-Freedom," in which he announced the death of free verse[40]. He went on to describe his "typographical revolution" which would use as many as four different colors of ink and twenty different type faces on a single page. These were not primarily intended to be used for ornamental purposes, but in order to enhance the meaning of the words and to give them a sense of motion. In reality, there are no known examples of Futurist poems that included four colors or twenty fonts[41]. But Marinetti definitely began using typography in a new way. His most famous poem, "Zang Tumb Tumb," was published as a book which included fold-out pages, different type faces, words printed diagonally or in circles, lines intersecting other lines, letters scattered around a page, as well as more traditional layouts. In one often-cited example, the poet Francesco Cangiullo "took the word 'fumare' ('to smoke'), lengthened it to 'FUUUUUMARE,' and made each successive letter larger so the word appeared to expand like a puff of smoke"[42].

Some Futurist poems added visual elements with the use of hand-drawn components, including illustrations incorporated into the body of the poem. As with collage, the line between literature and the visual arts was becoming less and less distinct.

"Destruction of Syntax" and a subsequent manifesto, "Geometrical and Mechanical Splendor and Sensitivity Toward Numbers"[43] described the concept of "multilinear lyricism" and various kinds of onomatopoeia. Words would be used to imitate sounds in realistic ways, using spelling and typography to emphasize this effect. For example, *ssiiiii* might represent the whistle of a tugboat[44]. Other kinds of onomatopoeia would use sounds in indirect or abstract ways to represent non-sound sensations and mental states.

Onomatopoeia in literature was certainly not a new idea. Most languages contain words like *hiss* and *buzz* which reproduce the sounds they describe. Repetition and rhythm are also common methods for imitating sounds. A well-known example of both of these kinds of onomatopoeia in poetry is Edgar Allan Poe's mid-19th century poem "The Bells"[45]. The kind of onomatopoeia which Marinetti described as "direct," in which invented words or non-words are used to imitate specific sounds, is also a very old technique in literature. Aristophanes used it more than 2000 years ago in his play *The Frogs*[46]. But Marinetti's use of creative spelling and typography to enhance the effect was new, and his use of abstract sounds within a poem to express feelings and mind-states was also original. His words-in-freedom syntax was a major departure from contemporary free verse, which still employed standard sentence structure and punctuation.

Although poetry remained the mainstay of Futurist literature, many authors also experimented with prose. Marinetti's novel, *Mafarka the Futurist*, was published in 1910. The main character was "an artificial man," in the form of "a cyborg-like flying machine that becomes a symbol of the new human being"[47]. The novel is generally described as racist, misogynistic, chaotic and intentionally offensive. Because of this book, Marinetti was tried for obscenity three times; he was acquitted once and given suspended sentences twice.

During his association with the Futurists, Palazzeschi wrote articles, short fiction, and two novels. *Man of Smoke*, published in 1911, is "an often hilarious and sometimes nightmarish social satire"[48] centered around a mysterious man made of smoke who comes to earth to bring an important message to mankind. Welcomed at first as a prophet and leader, he is eventually put on trial and imprisoned, but escapes in a wisp of smoke. The novel originally met with mixed reviews, but today it is considered "among the most original works of modern fiction"[49] and is one of very few works by Palazzeschi available in English.

Futurist Performance

Widely acknowledged today as the originators of performance art, the Futurists engaged in a constant series of public presentations. The publication of every new manifesto included readings on stage and other promotional events. Much of the new poetry was designed to be read aloud. In addition to painting and sculpture, members of the movement produced plays, music and film. There were eventually manifestoes on recitation, theater, dance, noise, cinema and music.

In 1869 the presentation of Alfred Jarry's pre-absurdist play *Ubu Roi* at the Theatre de l'Oeuvre in Paris had created a scandal when the audience, offended by the play's content and language, became chaotic and violent[50]. Inspired by Jarry, Marinetti opened his play *Le Roi Bombance* at the same theater in 1909, with similar results[51].

Starting in 1910, Futurist writers and artists, led by Marinetti, staged a series of Futurist evenings (*serate*) in cities throughout Italy. They rented lecture halls and theaters and advertised tickets for the opening night of a literary event. But the audiences did not get the well-behaved poetry readings they had anticipated. Michael and Victoria Kirby describe it this way:

> The attitude of the readers was arrogant, confident, energetic, and belligerent; they exchanged comments and insults with the spectators. The style of reading was loud and direct, making use of supporting noises and musical sounds. And the content of the manifestos was inflammatory: their programmatic rejection of the past and their exhortations to burn the libraries and flood the museums was enough . . . to infuriate most of the people in a country that was strongly oriented toward its artistic heritage[52].

Soon enough the audiences knew what to expect and came prepared with fruits and vegetables to throw at the performers. At one such evening, the painter Carlo Carrà shouted, "Throw an idea instead of potatoes, idiots!"[53]. Attacks from the audience were sometimes so severe that the performers were driven from the stage; in at least one instance, Marinetti had to be rescued by troops from a mob in the street[54]. Some Futurist events led to street fighting and arrests.

Provoking powerful reactions was part of the Futurist imperative. The first manifesto stated, "We intend to glorify aggressive action, a restive wakefulness, life at the double, the slap and the punching fist"[55] and "Art, indeed, can be nothing but violence, cruelty and injustice"[56]. And while they may have been annoyed by the vegetable assaults, at the same time they also invited strong responses from the audience. The evenings were deliberately designed to create an atmosphere of tension and irritation in the audience. For example, in one instance they sold twice as many tickets as there were seats[57]. In the 1913 manifesto on Variety Theater, Marinetti wrote about the importance of audience participation and suggested adding surprises in the form of pranks such as glue on the seats, sneezing powder, and providing free tickets to people known to be "a bit off their heads, irascible, or eccentric"[58].

Over time the productions became more elaborate, incorporating set decorations, costumes and lighting. Some evenings included displays of paintings and sculptures, as well as sounds or musical effects, along with scripted performances.

Marinetti and others wrote full-length plays and operas, but the most influential Futurist plays were short pieces known as *sintesi* (syntheses)[59]. "The Futurist Synthetic Theater," published by Marinetti, Emilio Settimelli and Bruno Corra in 1915, explained that futurist theater would be "Synthetic: That is, very brief. To compress into a few minutes, a few words and gestures, innumerable situations, sensibilities, ideas, sensations, facts and symbols"[60]. This philosophy is embodied in what is probably the shortest of the Futurist plays, Francesco Cangiullo's "Detonazione," which consists of nothing more than a bullet being fired[61]. *Futurist Performance*[62] includes the scripts of several of these short plays, translated into English. Many of them can be performed in two minutes or less.

The *serate* and the early theater productions were "primarily concerned with the relationship between the actor and the audience, and with political and ideological ideas to be expressed by the actor"[63]. But when Marinetti left the theater to go to war in 1915, Depero and Enrico Prampolini, both painters, took over with a different approach. They developed manifestos and theories that placed more emphasis on scenery, costumes, and the visual impact of a production. Prampolini even suggested using lights and colored gases dynamically to provide the audience with new kinds of sensations that would "render the actor unnecessary"[64]. In 1925 he received first prize for stage design at the International Exposition of Decorative Arts in Paris. His entry was a model of the Magnetic Theater, "a complicated construction of wheels, platforms, geometric solids, spheres and wires which were to 'replace the actors as focus for the performance'"[65]. It was "a completely abstract machine which would use space and mass, movement, light and sound to create a performance"[66].

In the early days of Futurist theater, the performers were the authors and their friends. But eventually it became necessary to hire actors. Between 1915 and 1920, several professional acting companies toured Italy in Futurist Synthetic Theater productions, presenting repertoires of plays that represented the contributions of more than fifty different authors[67]. The diversity of authorship and the wide latitude for interpretation and implementation of the concepts in the manifestoes meant that no single style prevailed. Some plays include sound effects or visual effects without dialogue. Some include non-human characters, such as airplanes, robots, animals and clouds, or characters that are abstract or symbolic, such as weather and colors. Others have human characters speaking and moving in a standard fashion. The dialogue may be recognizably conversational or may be filled with non-sequiturs, repetition, and nonsense. Some of the scripts were published using typography in the manner of the words-in-freedom poems, suggesting that they were intended for reading as much as performing.

Futurism and Lifestyle

City Life

The Futurists intended to influence all aspects of modern life, and with that in mind they published theories that asked for nothing less than a "Reconstruction of the Universe"[68]. Cities would have to be completely redesigned. In the 1914 "Manifesto of Futurist Architecture" [69] , Antonio Sant'Elia denounced all architecture since 1700 as an idiotic pastiche of poorly imitated historical styles. Futurist architecture would abolish elements that were purely decorative. It would reject anything traditional, classical or imitative. The emphasis would be on scientific and mathematical principals, using modern materials such as glass, reinforced concrete and steel. It would avoid horizontal and perpendicular lines, or shapes resembling cubes and pyramids, and would use instead lines that were "dynamic, oblique and elliptical"[70]. Between 1913 and 1914, Sant'Elia created a series of designs for "The New City", in which soaring, multi-level complexes integrated essential services, communication and transportation with urban life. No architectural plans were ever drawn up, but Sant'Elia had "considerable influence on the theory of subsequent architecture"[71]. He died in combat in 1916 at age 28.

According to Tisdall and Bozzolla, "The closest thing to a completely Futurist complex ever constructed in Italy was the Fiat-Lingotto factory in Turin, by Giacomo Matteo Trucco. This was built in 1919-1923 and featured multi-level workshops sunk into a raised racing track"[72].

Fashion

The 1910s marked the beginning of a period when clothing styles were gradually becoming simpler and more practical. During the 1920s and 30s, mass production and the development of synthetic fabrics helped make fashion more accessible to the general public. The faster pace of modern life, the changing nature of work, and the increasing participation of women in public society all demanded clothing that was comfortable and easy to care for.

Giacomo Balla wrote the "Futurist Manifesto of Men's Clothing" in 1913. He described current fashions as "tight-fitting, colorless, funereal . . . boring and unhygenic"[73]. He called for clothing in bright colors and dynamic designs, designed to last only a short time. Clothing would make people feel joyous and bring variety to life. Although he said clothing should be "comfortable and practical" he also suggested that it could be "lit by electric lamps"[74]. Balla began designing fabric and clothing with angular, asymmetrical lines and bold, geometric patterns. He had a suit made for himself in red, white and green (the colors of the Italian flag), and continued wearing his own designs into the 1930s. According to Emily Braun, his clothing designs were never mass-produced, but were manufactured by local tailors and his daughters[75]. Francesco Cangiullo wore one of the suits to a demonstration in Rome: "He jumped above the crowd in his red, white and green suit accompanied by a similarly colored beret crowned by a silver star. The appearance of this 'living flag' delighted the onlookers . . . . Cangiullo was later carried aloft in triumph by the throngs . . ."[76].

Most of the other Futurists seem to have been less adventurous when it came to personal fashion, although Marinetti, Depero and a few others sometimes wore bright ties or colorful vests designed by Depero, and Severini was once described as wearing open-toed shoes and mismatched socks[77].

In 1918, the designer Thayaht (pseudonym of Ernesto Michahelles) created a unisex garment he called the TuTa, which was intended to be easy to make at home from any available fabric. He had the design published in newspapers so that it could be used by everyone. Variations on the TuTa design are still in use, mostly as protective coveralls for workers. Thayaht went on to illustrate haute couture publications. Pippo Rizzo and other painters designed textiles, and Tullio Crali created designs for women's fashion. Depero had what was probably the widest impact through the "commercial viability of his designs for fashion boutiques, posters and the theater"[78].

Additional fashion manifestos included women's fashion in 1920, changes in men's fashion in 1932, and hats and ties in 1932 and 1933. The Futurists "anticipated much of the modern fashion phenomenon. Adapting to post-war economic realities and shifting class identities, they promulgated good design available to all through inexpensive materials . . . " and "correctly predicted the triumph of Italian style in the decades following World War II"[79].

Food

Marinetti's "Manifesto of Futurist Cuisine" appeared in 1930. He called for the establishment of a diet "in keeping with the increasingly airborne, faster pace of life"[80]. A better diet would support slimmer and more agile bodies, more positive emotions, a sharper intellect and greater creativity. The first step would be "to be rid of pasta, that idiotic gastronomic fetish of the Italians"[81]. Pasta, he felt, lacked nutritional value and was digested in an unhealthy way, leading to depression and laziness. Furthermore, the banishment of pasta would eliminate Italy's dependence on imported grain.

His hope was that science would eventually develop low-cost pills and powders that would provide all necessary nutrients and that could be supplied to workers by the state. Elimination of the need to spend money on food, combined with increased mechanization of manual labor, would make it possible to reduce the work day to two or three hours. The idea of a convenient meal in a pill is one that has reappeared in science fiction (and perhaps in the research departments of pharmaceutical companies) ever since.

Despite his call for ultra-efficient nutrition, Marinetti extolled the pleasures of dining. Music and poetry would accompany meals, while speeches and political discussions would be banned. Visual enjoyment would come from attractive table settings and food sculptures. Tactile pleasure would be increased by eating without utensils, and by touching objects of different textures while eating. By combining a dozen or more flavors, a single appetizer "will have the power to sum up a whole area of life, the development of a passionate affair, or an entire voyage to the Far East"[82]. Scientific equipment in the kitchen would ensure safe and healthful preparation.

In November 1930 Marinetti officially launched Futurist cuisine with a radio broadcast from a formal banquet at Milan's prestigious La Penna d'Oca restaurant. The Futurist restaurant, La Taverna del Santopalato (Tavern of the Holy Palate), opened around the same time. It lasted only about a year.

In 1932, Marinetti and Fillìa (pseudonym of Luigi Colombo) wrote *The Futurist Cookbook*. Many recipes called for towers of food, such as "Sculpted Meat," a tall cylinder of ground veal stuffed with eleven different vegetables, topped with honey and supported by a ring of sausages. The food as a work of art and the meal as an experience were more important than nutrition or even flavor, as suggested by a recipe called "The Excited Pig" in which a whole salami, cooked in espresso, is flavored with cologne[83]. In another recipe "Pieces of olive, fennel and kumquat are eaten with the right hand while the left hand caresses various swatches of sandpaper, velvet, and silk. At the same time the diner is blasted with a giant fan (preferably an airplane propeller) and nimble waiters spray him with the scent of carnation, to the strains of a Wagner opera"[84].

Clearly, this wasn't intended to be taken entirely seriously. *The Futurist Cookbook*'s "slapstick" and "goofy humor" has been likened to a cookbook produced by the Marx Brothers[85]. Marinetti acknowledged that some dishes might not be "appreciated by the needs of the stomach"[86] and that some might be better left uneaten. As performance art, Futurist cuisine was an inspiration to artists like Salvador Dali, who also created an offbeat cookbook and hosted Surrealist dinners. As food, some might see it as a forerunner of Nouvelle Cuisine, with its artistically assembled ingredients and juxtaposed flavors. But in the long run, Marinetti failed to predict the future of eating. As Jerry Adler points out:

> The factories and dynamos that the Futurists so admired gave birth to industrial food, which expresses its own ideology of efficiency and growth. Would the drive-through burger joint have seduced him with its energy and speed or repelled him with its bourgeois ordinariness? The latest culinary movement to emerge from Italy embraces a philosophy and a name that Marinetti would have reviled . . . Slow Food[87].

And More

The Futurists published hundreds of manifestos, articles, commentaries and pamphlets expanding on their theories and plans. Although the focus was usually on art, literature and performance, the overarching idea was that all of society needed to be changed and improved. In addition to the subjects discussed here, Futurist writings touched on a wide variety of topics, including household appliances, weights and measures, education, the beauty of machinery, marriage, and dancing. Many of these ideas remained just ideas, never fully explored or put into action.

Others led to real-world results, such as Depero's beautifully designed furniture and toys. But whatever the Futurists did, they were always hoping to get attention, stimulate change, and involve the public.

Summary

Italian Futurism was very much a product of its time and place. The social, political and intellectual atmosphere of Europe was generating excitement, upheaval, and all kinds of creative ideas. The past gave the Futurists something to rebel against. The present gave them motivation. All the different schools of thought that were developing around them were interacting and inspiring each other to go even farther and do even more. Futurism was often crazy and over the top, but it was the first organized avant-garde movement of the 20th century. It was also highly creative and original. It has unquestionably had a lasting impact that can still be seen today.

Notes

1 Berghaus xvii
2 Tisdall and Bozzolla 89
3 Berhause xviii
4 Belloli
5 Berghaus xxi
6 Humphreys 71
7 Humphreys 71
8 Berghaus xxv
9 Berghaus xxvi
10 Humphreys 72
11 Berghaus xxix
12 Blum 145
13 Humphreys 22
14 Apollonio 30
15 Apollonio 133
16 Perella and Stefanini x
17 Venn 9
18 Tisdall and Bozzolla 119
19 Hayward
20 Bohn 8
21 Kozloff ix
22 Kozloff 4
23 Marinetti 14-15
24 Apollonio 25-26
25 Apollonio 28
26 Within a year, Boccioni would reject Divisionism (Ottinger 130)
27 Apollonio 31
28 Apollonio 30
29 Ottinger 24
30 Lista 44
31 Apollonio 13
32 Poggi 1
33 Apollonio 65
34 "Parole in libertà" is variously translated as words in freedom, words in liberty, free words, and liberated words. I have used "words-in-freedom" here because this is how it appears most frequently in the works cited.
35 Bohn 6
36 Jones 186
37 Marinetti 107-119
38 Marinetti 113

[39] Folejewski 33
[40] Marinetti 124
[41] Cundy 349
[42] Bohn 7
[43] Marinetti 135-142
[44] Marinetti 140
[45] Poe 764
[46] Benet 719
[47] Marrone 1718
[48] Italica
[49] Perella and Stefanini xi
[50] Goldberg 10
[51] Kirby 13
[52] Kirby 14
[53] Goldberg 12
[54] Kirby 16
[55] Marinetti 13
[56] Marinetti 16
[57] Tisdall and Bozzolla 92
[58] Marinetti 190
[59] Kirby 41
[60] Apollonio 184
[61] Gordon 353
[62] Kirby
[63] Taylor 57
[64] Taylor 60
[65] Taylor 69
[66] Taylor 70
[67] Gordon 354
[68] Apollonio 197
[69] Apollonio 160
[70] Tisdall and Bozzolla 130
[71] Tisdall and Bozzolla 132
[72] Tisdall and Bozzolla 135
[73] Apollonio 132
[74] Apollonio 133
[75] Braun 36
[76] Braun 36-37
[77] Ottinger 28
[78] Lehmann 119
[79] Braun 38
[80] Marinetti 395
[81] Marinetti 395

[82] Marinetti 398
[83] Perrottet
[84] Perrottet
[85] Perrottet
[86] Adler
[87] Adler

Works Cited

Adler, Jerry. "Back to the Future." *The New Yorker* 6 September 2004: 101. General Onefile. Web. Retrieved 7 Oct. 2010.

Apollonio, Umbo, ed. *Futurist Manifestos.* Boston: MFA, 2001.

Belloli, Carlo. "About this Artist." *MoMa: The Collection.* Web. Retrieved 4 Oct. 2010.

Benét's Reader's Encyclopedia. New York: Harper, 1987.

Berghaus, Günther. Introduction and Notes. In Marinetti xvii-xxix and 423-510.

Blum, Cinzia Sartini. *The Other Modernism: F.T. Marinetti's Futurist Fiction of Power.* Berkeley: University of California Press, 1996.

Bohn, Willard. *Italian Futurist Poetry.* Toronto: University of Toronto Press, 2005.

Braun, Emily. "Futurist Fashion: Three Manifestoes." Art Journal 54.1 (1995): 34-41.

Cundy, David. "Marinetti and Italian Futurist Typography." *Art Journal* Winter 1981: 349-352.

Folejewski, Zbigniew. *Futurism and its Place in the Development of Modern Poetry.* Ottawa: University of Ottawa Press, 1980.

Goldberg, Rosalee. *Performance.* New York: Abrams, 1979.

Goldberger, Paul. "Architecture: Antonio Sant'Elia." New York Times, 21 Feb. 1986: C24.

Gordon, R.S. "The Italian Futurist Theatre" A Reappraisal." Modern Language Review 85:2 (1990): 349-361.

Hayward, James. CD liner notes for *Musica Futurista: The Art of Noise.* LTM Recordings. Web. 8 Nov. 2010.

Humphreys, Richard. *Futurism.* Cambridge: Cambridge UP, 1999.

Italica Press website. Web. Retrieved 22 Nov. 2010.

Jones, P.M. "Influence of Walt Whitman on the Origin of the 'Vers Libre'." *Modern Language Review* April 1916: 186-194.

Kirby, Michael and Victoria Nes Kirby. *Futurist Performance*. New York: Paj, 1986.

Kozloff, Max. *Cubism/Futurism*. New York: Charterhouse, 1973.

Lehmann, Ulrich."Futurist Fashion, Italian." *Encyclopedia of Clothing and Fashion*. Ed. Valerie Steele. Detroit: Scribner's, 2005.

Lista, Giovanni. "The Italian Sources of Futurism." In Ottinger 42-51.

Marinetti, F.T. *Critical Writings*. Trans. Doug Thompson. Ed. Günther Berghaus. New York: Farrar, 2006.

Marrone, Gaetana, ed. *Encylopedia of Italian Literary Studies*. New York: Taylor & Francis Group, 2007.

Ottinger, Didier, ed. *Futurism*. Paris: Editions du Centre Pompidou, 2009.

Perella, Nicholas J. and Ruggero Stefanini, trans. and eds. *Introduction. Man of Smoke*. By Aldo Palazzeschi. New York: Italaca Press, 1992.

Perrottet, Tony. "The Futurist Cookbook." *Table Matters*. Web. Retrieved 24 Nov. 2010.

Poe, Edgar Allan. *Complete Stories and Poems*. Garden City: Doubleday, 1966.

Poggi, Christine. In Defiance of Painting: Cubism, Futurism, and the Invention of Collage. New Haven: Yale UP, 1992.

Taylor, Christiana J. *Futurism*. Ann Arbor MI: University Microfilms International, 1974.

Tisdall, Caroline and Angelo Bozzolla. *Futurism*. New York: Oxford UP, 1978.

Venn, Edward. "Rethinking Russolo." Tempo 64 (2010): 8-16.